COLORING BOOK

_____

_____

_____

TEST YOUR COLORS HERE

1920 Rolls Royce Silver Ghost

1935 Chevrolet Suburban

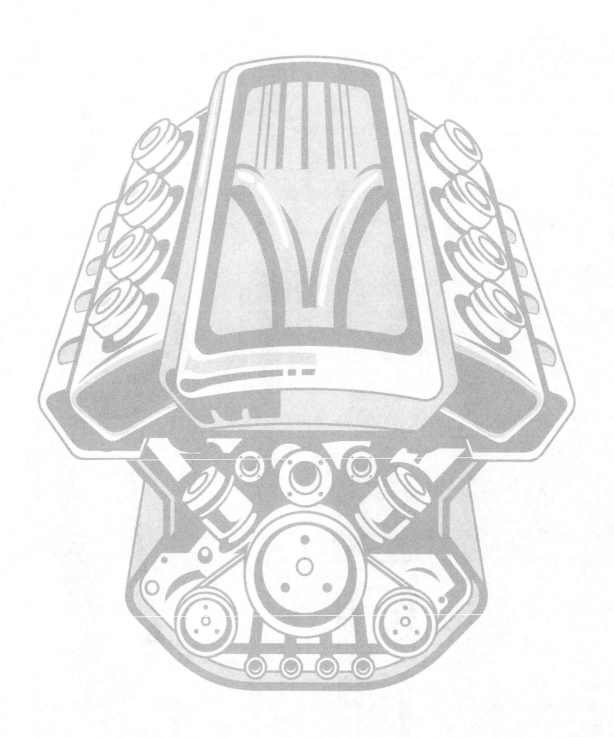

1959 Cadillac Deville

1940 Chrysler New Yorker

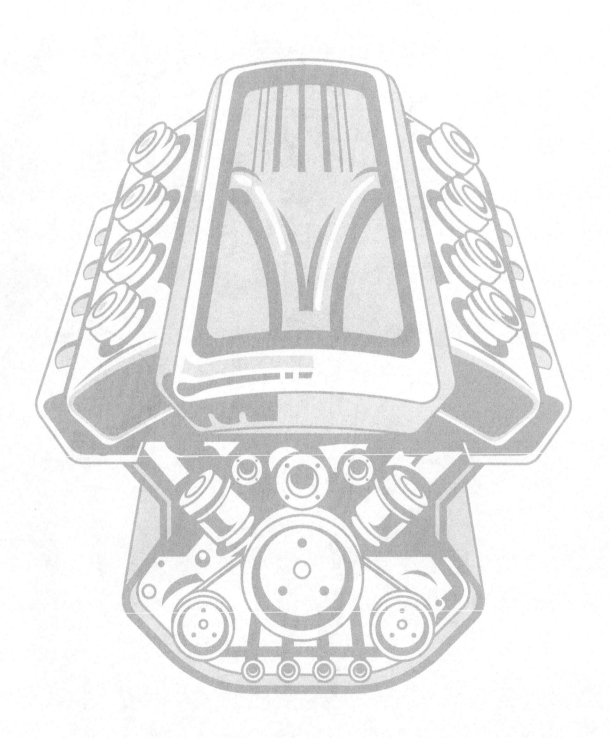

1945 Dodge Power Wagon

1949 Ford F Series

1949 Oldsmobile 88

1970 Oldsmobile Cutlass

1949 Chevrolet 3100

1934 Packard Super Eight

1962 Cadillac Series 62

1970 Toyota Land Cruiser

1953 Buick Skylark

1953 Ford F100

1954 Hudson Hornet

1966 Volvo P1800

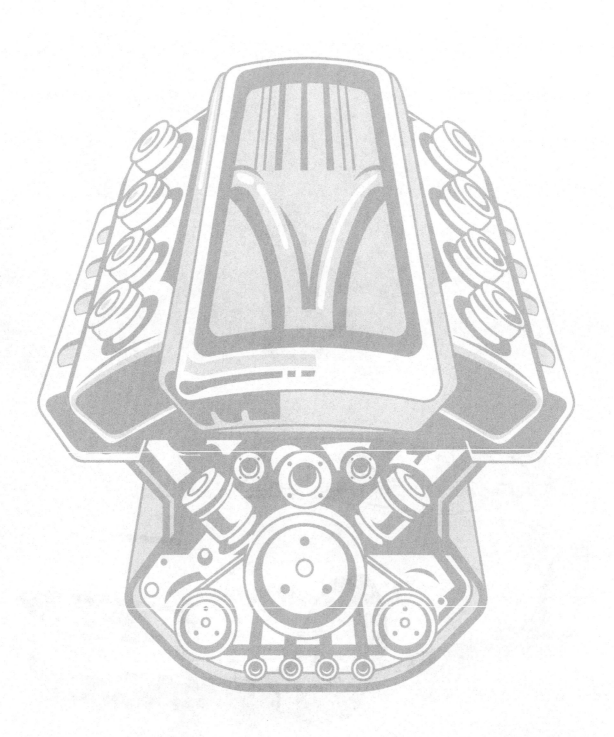

1956 Lamborghini Miura

1956 Oldsmobile Rocket 88

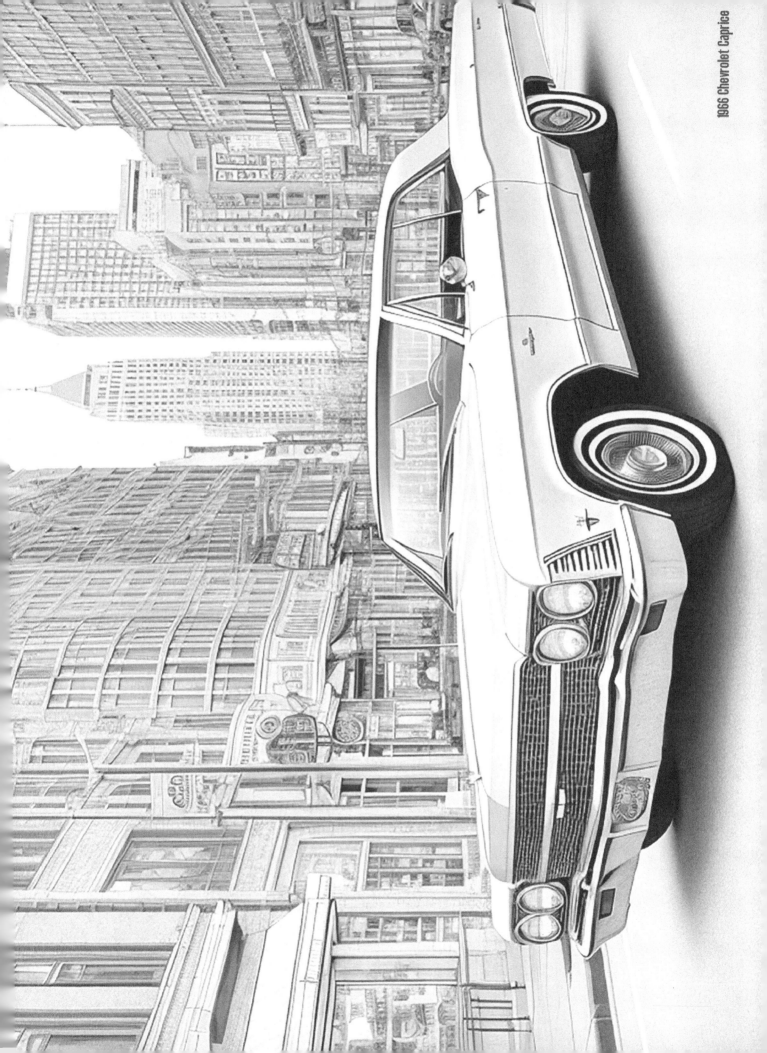
1966 Chevrolet Caprice

1957 Chevrolet Task Force

1957 Mercedes Benz 300SL

1935 Chrysler Airflow

1959 GMC Blue Chip

1969 Pontiac GTO

1961 Chevrolet Impala

1961 Lincoln Continental

1950 Dodge B Series

1962 Ferrari 250 GTO

1964 Aston Martin DB5

1964 Ford Mustang

1965 Dodge D Series

1957 Chevrolet Bel Air

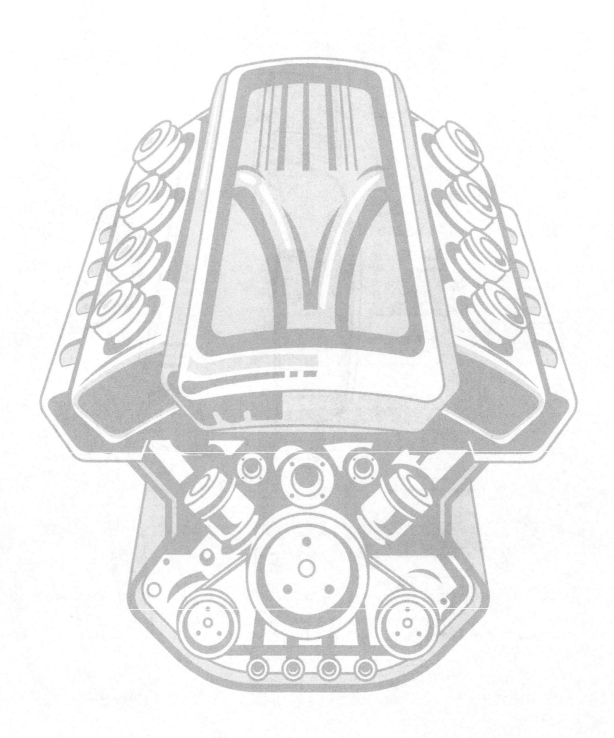

1966 Ford GT40

1955 Ford Thunderbird

1967 Buick Riviera

1967 Chevrolet Camaro SS

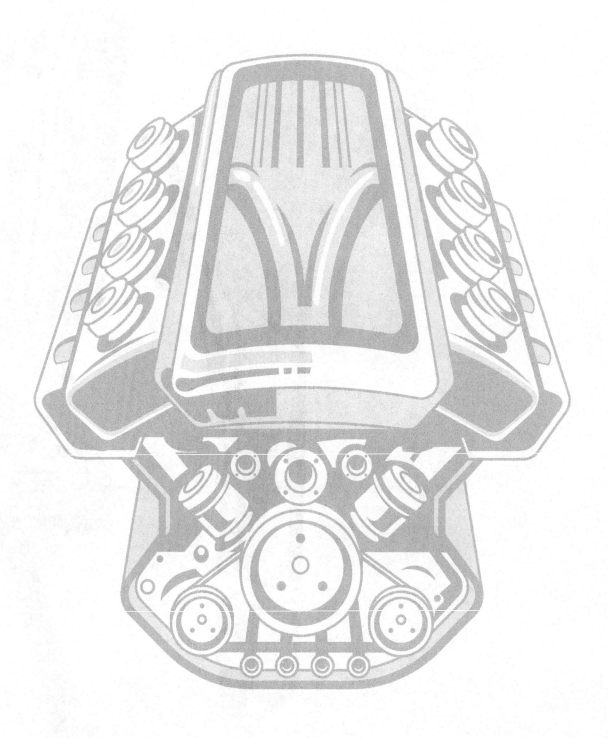

1968 Chevrolet Corvette Stingray

1969 Dodge Challenger

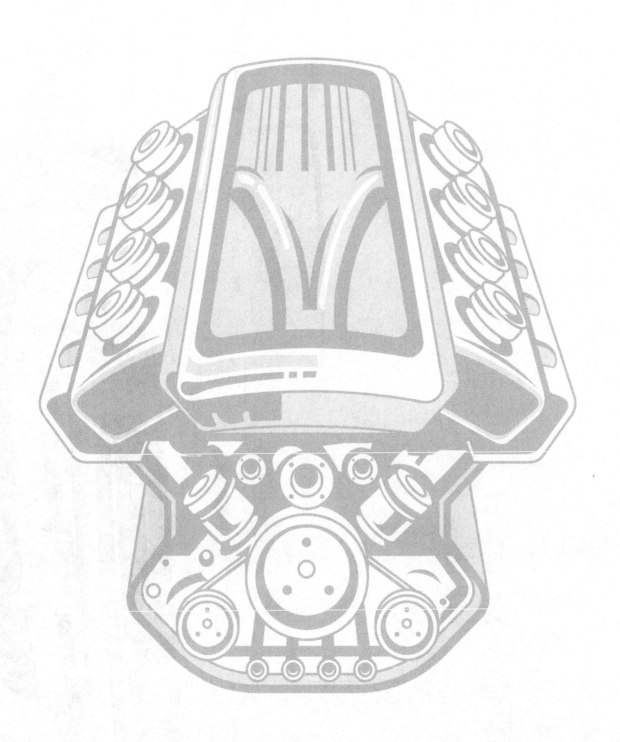

1961 Chevrolet CK

1970 Chevrolet El Camino

1970 Ford Bronco

1949 Oldsmobile 88

1970 Porsche 911

1951 GMC 100

1971 Plymouth Barracuda

1972 Dodge Charger

1972 Volkswagen Beetle

1975 Jeep Wrangler

1955 Plymouth Fury

Made in the USA
Columbia, SC
19 September 2025